CAMPING BASICS

by Wayne Armstrong

Illustrations by
Robert Schoolcraft

With Photographs

Created and Produced by
Arvid Knudsen

PRENTICE-HALL, Inc.

Englewood Cliffs, New Jersey

Dedication

*To our wonderful family camping days
and to those to come.*

Other Sports Basics Books in Series

BASKETBALL BASICS *by Greggory Morris*
RUNNING BASICS *by Carol Lea Benjamin*
DISCO BASICS *by Maxine Polley*
GYMNASTICS BASICS *by John and Mary Jean Traetta*
RACQUETBALL BASICS *by Tony Boccaccio*
FRISBEE DISC BASICS *by Dan Roddick*
SWIMMING BASICS *by Rob Orr and Jane B. Tyler*
HORSEBACK RIDING BASICS *by Dianne Reimer*
SKIING BASICS *by Al Morrozzi*
BASEBALL BASICS *by Jack Lang*
FISHING BASICS *by John Randolph*
FOOTBALL BASICS *by Larry Fox*
SOCCER BASICS *by Alex Yannis*
SAILING BASICS *by Lorna Slocombe*
BICYCLING BASICS *by Tim and Glenda Wilhelm*
BACKPACKING BASICS *by John Randolph*
TENNIS BASICS *by Robert J. LaMarche*
TRACK & FIELD BASICS *by Fred McMane*
HOCKEY BASICS *by Norman MacLean*
BOWLING BASICS *by Chuck Pezzano*
KARATE BASICS *by Thomas J. Nardi*
ICE-SKATING BASICS *by Norman MacLean*
WATERSPORTS BASICS *by Don Wallace*
CAMPING BASICS *by Wayne Armstrong*
BOATING BASICS *by Henry F. Halsted*

Text copyright © 1985 by Wayne Armstrong and
Arvid Knudsen
Illustrations copyright © 1985 by Arvid Knudsen

Book design by Arvid Knudsen

Printed in the United States of America   · J

Prentice-Hall International (UK) Limited, London
Prentice-Hall of Australia, Pty. Ltd., Sydney
Prentice-Hall of Canada, Inc., Toronto
Prentice-Hall Hispanoamericana, S.A., Mexico
Prentice-Hall of India Private Ltd., New Delhi
Prentice-Hall of Japan, Inc., Tokyo
Prentice-Hall of Southeast Asia Pte. Ltd., Singapore
Whitehall Books Limited, Wellington, New Zealand
Editora Prentice-Hall do Brasil Ltda., Rio de Janeiro

10 9 8 7 6 5 4 3 2 1

Library of Congress Cataloging in Publication Data

Armstrong, Wayne.
    Camping basics.

    Summary: Outlines the skills, equipment,
precautions, and safety measures for various
camping situations.
    1. Camping—Juvenile literature. [1. Camping]
I. Schoolcraft, Robert, ill. II. Title.
GV191.7.A75   1985   796.54   85-9407
ISBN 0-13-112657-1

CONTENTS

*Photos on pps. 4, 6, 8, 14, 16, 28, 38, 40 courtesy
of* Coleman Company, Inc.

INTRODUCTION

Let's go camping!

Ever since I was a boy, those words have been magic. And now they call up memories of sleeping out under a tree in the pasture on an Illinois farm where I grew up; of the cabin our Boy Scout troop built in the woods along the Illinois River near a spot where Marquette and Joliet camped in 1763 on their way back north after exploring the Mississippi; of camping with my children in the Great Smoky Mountains the time a bear robbed our ice chest; of the crab we trapped in a tidal pool on the Maine coast; of a mother loon and her chicks on a lake in the north woods of Canada; of hummingbirds feeding at our camp in the Colorado Rockies.

Camping means the sound of birds waking you at dawn, the smell of wood smoke in the bright morning air, the aroma of breakfast cooking on an open fire, the warmth of a fire on a cool evening, stars so bright you think you can touch them, the sound of rain on your tent when you're warm and snug in your sleeping bag.

Camping means sharing all those experiences with friends and family—and the sharing increases the enjoyment, creating shared memories that will stay with you for years.

Let's go camping!

1. A SHORT HISTORY

I like to think of camping as our oldest sport. The Neanderthal family, some 40,000 years ago, was a camping family, although they probably didn't appreciate how lucky they were to be able to camp out all the time. American Indians were all originally campers. Although many tribes over the years built permanent dwellings and some (such as the pueblo-building tribes of the Southwest) built elaborate multistoried cities, most of the Plains tribes were still "campers" in 1803 when Lewis and Clark explored the Missouri— camping. The Mountain Men who first explored the West, the French *voyageurs* who developed the fur trade in the Canadian Northwest, the pioneers on the Oregon Trail, the forty-niners heading for California to dig for gold, the cowboys trail-herding toward Dodge City —all were campers.

Those people camped because they had to; but there always have been those who camped just because they wanted to. Henry David Thoreau was a camper and wrote about it in *The Maine Woods*. John Muir was a camper and was largely responsible for preserving some of the most beautiful camping areas in the West. President Theodore Roosevelt was a camper and started our magnificent National Park system. There were a great many others less well known, but most people were limited to camping quite near to where they lived. Roads were pretty bad; transportation was slow; equipment was primitive. But after the turn of the century, cars improved, new roads were built, and people became more mobile. More of them went camping, and they went farther and more often.

7

EVERYONE PITCHES IN TO HELP IN FAMILY CAMPING.

Probably the first organized campers were the Boy Scouts, Girl Scouts, and Camp Fire Girls. Scouting started in England in 1908 and came to the United States in 1910; the Camp Fire Girls organization started the same year. Since then there have been several million members of these groups, most of whom have enjoyed one or more types of camping experience. And since young campers grow up, become parents, and take their children camping, camping as a family activity has grown steadily in popularity.

In economic terms, campers were a growing market, so more camping facilities were built and better equipment was manufactured to meet their needs. And then more people went camping. This has caused a steady growth in the availability of camping facilities, and there are now thousands of public and private campgrounds to choose from, ranging from primitive areas deep in the wilderness to very fancy establishments near the edges of large cities.

You, too, can be a camper and share the fun of living out-of-doors!

2. WHY GO CAMPING?

A friend of mine, in whose mind "roughing it" means staying in a resort hotel that has only a black-and-white TV, once told me I was crazy to leave my nice, modern, comfortable house to go out in the woods and sleep in a tent! He said the human race had spent ten thousand years inventing the modern kitchen and it was stupid to go back to cooking over an open fire.

So why do we campers camp? Probably there are as many reasons as there are campers. Our family enjoys learning about plants and animals and birds, in addition to the fun of just being out in the woods, by a lake, or in the mountains. We always carry Peterson's Field Guides to birds, plants, and trees and try to identify the things we see around our camp and on our hikes. And we carry binoculars to help us see the birds and animals more clearly. What better way to learn about nature? No one really can tell you what it feels like to have a mother raccoon lead her family through your campsite while you're eating lunch. How can you put into words the thrill of watching a pair of beavers repairing their dam? You have to experience it directly.

But learning *about* nature isn't the only reward; you also learn to *appreciate* nature and how to take care of our planet Earth. The more you know about our natural environment and how complicated and fragile it really is, the more you learn to treasure it and want to preserve it. You and I can enjoy the natural beauties of our country because John Muir and Theodore Roosevelt and others like them fought to preserve the wilderness for us. We must protect it for our own children and grandchildren.

One of the greatest rewards of camping, I think, is something that happens inside you. As you become more self-reliant—and camping can certainly teach you skills that will increase your ability to take care of yourself under a wide variety of circumstances—you become more self-confident. Your self-esteem increases, and you develop an awareness of your own abilities—and limitations. Camping can help you to become a more responsible, self-assured person.

Don't overlook the value and the fun of gaining new experiences, seeing different parts of the country, making new friends from different places. We live in a very big country with many different kinds of climate and many people with different traditions and customs; yet most of us spend our lives within a very small circle, never seeing how others live. Camping can be a most enjoyable way of broadening your horizons—of learning about other places and other people.

3. WHAT DO YOU DO IN CAMP?

I'm always surprised when people ask me, as some do, what we do in camp. The tone of the question often seems to imply that there isn't anything *to* do. That has never been my problem; I have trouble finding time to do all the things I want to do.

In most organized group camps—such as Scout camps, Y camps, or the special "theme" camps we'll discuss later, the programs are often group programs, laid out by the camp directors and counselors. Camps vary in size, of course, and in the degree to which they organize the campers' time. In some camps, a camper is quite free to follow an individual schedule; in others, many of the activities are planned for you, and you might even complain that you haven't enough free time. You will have free time, of course, for reading, for getting acquainted with new friends, for writing those post cards saying "Wish you were here"—but your time will be well organized.

Typically, group campers will sleep in a bunk house or dormitory-type building. They'll be awakened pretty early in the morning—6:30 or 7:00—and have about half an hour to wash up, brush teeth, make the bed, and get ready for breakfast. Breakfast is usually a group meal and, since young campers have big appetites, a hearty one. At many camps, the campers themselves take turns serving the meals and helping clean up the dining hall afterward.

After breakfast, the morning activities begin. Depending on the kind of camp, these could be hiking, swimming (with instruction for beginners), canoeing (again, with beginners' instruction), riding, tennis, baseball, arts and crafts, music, or (at Scout camps) working on scouting skills and the merit badges that show the skills mastered. At many camps, a number of these activities will go on at the same time in different areas of the camp, giving the camper a choice of activities to participate in each day. Usually these activities are supervised by the camp counselors, who try to help each camper gain the most in enjoyment or increased skill from the activity.

After lunch, which again will be a group meal (unless some campers are on an all-day hike or trip away from the camp area), afternoon activities begin. Often this will be a continuation of the morning program. At other camps, the afternoons are less structured and provide free time for individual activities. (This is when you can write your post cards.)

After the evening meal—almost always a group meal that everybody attends—most group camps have an evening program. Frequently, this is a gathering around a large campfire, often with songs and entertainment by the campers. Many who have attended group camps find that the "campfire" is the high point of their time at camp.

The range of activities available in group camping is wide because there are so many types of camps available; but it is in family camping that the range of activities really opens up. In fact, the activities available are limited only by your own imagination and the time and money available.

Since you're camping by yourself, without a group to help you do what has to be done, one of the first and most important things to do is to set up and maintain the campsite. After you become experienced, this becomes pretty routine, but it is always good to have a well-set-up camp, with the tent and cooking areas conveniently arranged. Learning how to set up a proper camp is important. And maintaining an orderly camp is not only necessary if one is to be a responsible camper, but it makes the cooking and eating (and the inevitable dishwashing) more convenient—and enjoyable. Besides that, tending the fire and keeping the camp neat can be fun in itself.

But apart from the mechanics of setting up and breaking camp, there are many other activities possible. We do a lot of hiking when we camp. We take long bird-watching walks. And, since I'm an enthusiastic photographer, I go on hikes looking for just the right scenery to shoot.

Photo by Wayne Armstrong.

HIKING AND EXPLORING IS A FAVORITE GROUP
CAMPING ACTIVITY.

We take a canoe with us when we camp, since most of the time we look for places near lakes and streams. Canoeing is an enjoyable part of our camping experience. So is fishing. On one wall of our house is a stuffed lake trout 30 inches long that my son caught on a lake in Canada. On one of our trips, we went horseback riding. My son and I once climbed a 13,000-foot mountain in Colorado. Out West, we went to a rodeo. We swam and collected seashells on Cape Cod. Another time, we went down into the Grand Canyon. In California, we took a sailplane ride along the edge of the Sierra Nevada.

Short backpacking "overnighters" from a base campsite add to the fun of camping. Learning to read maps and use a compass increase your self-reliance in the wilderness. ("Orienteering" is the name for training trips designed especially to teach these skills.) Learning to cook out-of-doors presents unique challenges and great satisfactions—not to mention good food.

And don't overlook just plain ordinary sightseeing. A great many camping areas are close to places of interest. You can camp at the Grand Canyon; near Disneyland; at the edge of Boston; near the Gettysburg battlefield; at the Carlsbad Caverns; within sight of the Empire State Building; just outside Washington, D.C.; close to Williamsburg, Virginia; near Cape Kennedy. From your campsite base, you can make day trips to some of the most popular tourist attractions in the country.

Of course, many of the activities I've mentioned for family camping also are possible for group campers, too.

So, what can you do in camp? Just about anything you can do anywhere else, if you use your imagination. But be prepared for the unexpected. We always take along a bag of books to read. It does occasionally rain, even in California. Lying in your tent with a good book is a fine way to spend a wet afternoon. You might want to take table games such as Scrabble and Trivial Pursuit and a deck of cards for the evenings.

4. DECISIONS! DECISIONS! DECISIONS!

Campers today have a great many options available to them in deciding their camping experience. An early decision to make might be, ''What kind of camping do you want?''

What Type of Camping?

There are three general types of camping: (1) the organized group camps such as Campfire Girls and Scout camps, Y camps, and camps affiliated with religious organizations; (2) commercially operated camps, many of them theme camps specializing in some particular activity, such as swimming, horseback riding—even weight loss; and (3) the broad area of family camping. Family camping would include day-camping (very much like a picnic) and weekending (a two-day trip to a nearby camping area), as well as longer vacation trips of one or two weeks during which a family group might travel a considerable distance from home. Each type of camping has its own special requirements and its own special rewards.

Group Camps

''Going to camp'' has been a treasured experience for thousands of boys and girls. For many campers, the Campfire Girls, the Scout camp, or the Y camp gave them their first taste of outdoor

THIS FAMILY HAS A DOME STYLE TENT.

life. They learned the basic camping skills and the art of living with and getting along with other boys and girls, under the guidance of experienced camp counselors. For many people, the memories of singing in the evening around the campfire last a lifetime.

If you are a Scout or a member of a Y or know someone who is, you can get information about these group camps in your area by asking the Scoutmaster or someone at the information desk at the Y. If you don't have a Scout troop or a Y near you, you can find the addresses of these organizations in the Appendix. Many religious groups also have summer camps, and your minister, priest, or rabbi may be able to tell you how to find out more about them.

Most camps provide detailed pamphlets showing locations, schedules, activities, and fees. The Peterson directory listed in the Appendix gives brief information of this type, but you also should contact the particular camp you're interested in for their brochures. Read the pamphlets carefully so that you won't be disappointed. Is swimming important to you? Then you may want to choose a camp on a lake. Is hiking in the woods something you want very much to do? Check to see the nature of the landscape of the camp you're considering.

There are important questions you must ask about what you will have to bring with you. Camp pamphlets will tell you whether you have to bring your own bedding and towels. Most camps will provide the sport and recreation equipment you will need, but generally you will have to bring your own sport clothing—swimsuit, hiking shoes, tennis shorts, and the like.

Your parents will want to know, of course, what medical supervision is available at the camp. You also will want to be sure that you have any needed vaccinations and that you get them early enough. (If you're taking any medication, be sure that you check with your doctor before you go and advise the camp counselor when you arrive.)

An important question, of course, is the *cost* of going to camp. As you can imagine, the cost can vary a great deal. Some Scout camps charge as little as $1 per person per day if the group brings its own food and does its own cooking. For those using the complete facilities of the camp, the per-person charge probably will be somewhere around $100–125 per week. Commercially operated camps, however, will cost more, and some theme camps can be

TENNIS

GOLF

SWIMMING

HORSEBACK RIDING

Some camp activities.

quite expensive. But there is often "scholarship" help available. Your local Y or Scout council, or your local church or synagogue could help you find out what is possible in your area.

Theme Camps

There are hundreds of camps that concentrate most of their attention on a particular area of interest. I call these theme camps. For example, there are tennis camps where most of the outdoor activity is devoted to learning and playing tennis, frequently under the direction of a professional tennis player. There are sailing camps located on the seashore or on a lake where you can learn the skills of handling sailboats of various sizes and under various conditions, all under the direction of experienced sailors. There are camps concentrating on horseback riding, where you can learn to ride if you're a novice or improve your skills if you already know how to ride. There are camps concentrating on golf, weight loss, baseball, computers, drama, canoeing, dance, winter sports, science. There are music camps and wilderness survival camps and camps where you can learn a foreign language. And, of course, there are many camps for those who just want to get out in the country to swim, hike, and enjoy being out-of-doors.

There also are organized camping trips devoted to special activities—such as photography; white-water canoeing; bird-watching; orienteering, or packing into the deep wilderness such as the back country of the Grand Tetons in Wyoming.

Whatever your interest, you can find a camp that will suit you. In other words, if you *can* do it or want to learn, someone probably has started camps *where* you can do it! You just have to find them.

I haven't found any single place listing all of the specialty camps in any given area. The directories listed in the Appendix will give you some information, but if you want a camp that specializes in your area of interest, these directories may not give you enough information. Again, your local Scoutmaster or the people at the Y may have lists of the specialty camps in your vicinity. Each Sunday, the back pages of *The New York Times Magazine* carry advertisements for camps, mostly in the eastern part of the country but in many other areas as well. Other major city newspapers have similar

Types of theme camps that are advertised in newspapers and magazines.

21

advertising sections. Naturally, there are more ads in the spring of the year when people are planning their summer activities, but camping is a year-round activity.

Your local sporting goods store probably can give you information about camps specializing in certain sports. For instance, a store with a good business in tennis equipment probably will know about the tennis camps in your area. If you're already heavily into a certain activity, you may possibly be in touch with local groups interested in that activity. They can help you find the camps for your interest. In other words, ask questions.

If you have decided you want to consider a specialized camp, you then have the same kinds of questions to answer as the group campers. What do you have to bring with you? What does it cost? Is there scholarship assistance available? What kind of instruction or supervision is available? Is the camp suitable for the level of skill you have attained in the activity? For example, a particular tennis camp may be aimed toward those who have already become very good players; they may not have classes or instruction for beginners. These are questions you will have to ask.

And, again, your parents will want to know the kind of camp supervision that is available and the nature of the medical facilities available in the case of an accident. This is very important in those camps devoted to strenuous sports. Many camps are accredited by the American Camping Association. This means that they have met the standards of this association in terms of facilities, supervision, hygiene, safety, and so on. Many advertisements will indicate if the camp has been accredited. You can write or call the A.C.A. (the address and phone number are listed in the Appendix) to learn if a particular camp has been accredited.

Family Camps

In the past 20 or 30 years, more and more people are living in cities and suburbs. And as the cities have grown, people have had to travel ever greater distances to find open country. As a result, fewer and fewer people have had a chance to experience the natural beauty of our country. Camping has become an increasingly popular way for families to become acquainted with the out-of-doors and with each other, and to explore the country at modest expense. Camping costs a lot less than staying in motels and eating in restaurants. (I think it's a lot more fun.) There is also an enormous range of possibilities available—in geography, in types of camping, in equipment, in the level of comforts—so that each family or individual can choose just about any style of camping desired.

For our purposes here, we'll consider that family camping includes all the kinds of camping people do by themselves or with family members or friends. Since this has been my kind of camping for the past 25 years and since most needed information about group and specialty camps can be obtained from the directories listed in the Appendix or from the camps themselves, most of this book will be devoted to family camping.

Where to Go?

After you and your family have decided what type of camping you want to do, you've got another decision to make: Where do you want to go? Do you want to go to the seashore or to the mountains? To the woods or to a lake or to the desert? The amount of time you have may determine where you go, by limiting how far you *can* go. After all, you won't want to spend all of your available time just getting there.

Forests, lakes, seashore, mountains, and desert areas are all available for camping, and each different environment has its own attractions. (Its own limitations, too. It's difficult to do much surfing in the Rockies, and the mountain climbing isn't very exciting on Cape Cod!)

As the types of activities available will vary with the different environments, so too will the requirements placed on the camper in terms of equipment and physical conditioning.

Forests and Lakes

Forest and lake camping is what most people think of when they think of camping. Canoes, fishing poles, and walking through the woods come to mind. We camped once on the Upper Peninsula of Michigan, near Tahquamenon Falls. Our 12-year-old son had the time of his life hiking along wooded trails in "Hiawatha country" and walking across the river *behind* the falling water. One summer, camped on a little lake near Baxter Park in Maine, our two boys spent hours on the lake "practicing" capsizing the canoe and then refloating it. And 13-year-old Dave caught a 30-inch lake trout from that same canoe on a little lake in Ontario. Lake and forest camping often can be combined—in the Adirondacks, for example, and in places like Minnesota's northern woods.

This kind of camping gives you lots of opportunities for fishing, swimming, hiking, and birdwatching. It's probably the least demanding in terms of necessary equipment; and unless the woods you camp in are in very hilly or mountainous terrain, forest camping should present no special requirements for physical conditioning. Forest trails for hiking in northern Michigan, Wisconsin, Minnesota, and the rest of the Midwest are pretty level. Any reasonably healthy young person will find such areas manageable. On the other hand, camping in the Quetico—the canoe wilderness along the route

CAMPING AND FISHING GO NATURALLY TOGETHER.

of the *voyageurs* between Minnesota and western Ontario—can require some rather strenuous portaging. If you follow their trails, which are still clearly visible, you'll learn that those old *voyageurs* were in pretty good condition.

Seashore and Desert

Seashore camping can present a pretty mixed bag: the Gulf coast and most of the East coast are generally low-lying areas; the coast of New England and the West coast are much more rugged and in some areas quite mountainous. What they have in common is the opportunity for swimming (although the water off New England can be pretty cold), boating, and the exploration of the animal life along the shoreline. We've had great fun digging for clams on tidal flats in the Northeast. We found a crab trapped in a tidal pool when the tide went out in Maine—but our 13-year-old daughter wouldn't let us eat it. Our eldest daughter spent hours on the beach in Florida feeding popcorn, one kernel at a time, to sea gulls that swooped down to pluck it from her hand.

Seashore and desert camping present quite different opportunities for exploring the habitats of birds and animals. Both salt-water marshes and deserts have a wonderful variety of wildlife. Desert wildlife is, of course, much more difficult to watch—desert animals are more apt to come out at night when it's cool. But there are many varieties of birds and plants to see. I remember once when we watched a small brown bird, perhaps a cactus wren, carrying bugs to its young in a hole in a tall cactus.

These areas also will make varying demands on you in terms of your physical condition. Just as there are great differences between the flat coast of Florida and the rugged coastline of Oregon, there are great differences in deserts. For example, there is more than a mile difference in the altitude of California's Mojave Desert and that of the high deserts of northern Arizona. The thing to remember about deserts is that they are dangerous if you are unprepared for the wide changes in temperature between noon and midnight or if you hike without sufficient water.

Mountains

Mountain camping offers still different hiking challenges and can demand strenuous physical activity. There are two major groups of mountains in the United States—the eastern mountains of the Appalachian chain and the great mass of western mountains that often are lumped together into one group called the Rockies. The eastern mountains are older mountains; time and weather have worn them down. They generally are lower, more heavily wooded, and the slopes are less steep than the newer, more rugged mountains of the West. The highest mountains in the East are little more than a mile high, while there are many peaks in the West that approach or exceed three miles. One summer in Colorado, my 16-year-old son climbed to the top of 12,000-foot-high Baker Mountain, while I puffed along behind him and finally gave up at about 10,000 feet. I wasn't in good enough condition to make the top. Obviously, physical activity in the western mountains presents different physical conditioning than in the lower, more heavily wooded Appalachian chain. But there are also different rewards. My daughter coaxed feeding hummingbirds to sit on her finger; mountain trout somehow taste better than their lowland cousins; breakfast smells better in the thin mountain air.

There are even some wonderful places where you can combine the seashore and the mountains. Acadia National Park in Maine is one such place. One day our kids climbed about on the shore rocks hunting for crabs and clams in the morning and then after lunch climbed the 1,000-foot "precipice" on Cadillac Mountain. One morning we got up at 4:00 A.M. and sat, wrapped in our sleeping bags, atop Cadillac Mountain to see the sun come up over the Atlantic. We were the first people in the United States to see the sun that morning!

Which Camp to Choose?

After you decide the type of camping you want and the area you wish to visit, you then will have to decide which particular camp you want to go to. In almost all areas, there will be too many camps for you to contact all of them. But you do need to know what services and facilities the various camps offer.

There are a number of very comprehensive campground directories. You'll find some of them listed in the Appendix. You may be able to find others in your local library under the catalog card heading "Camping Directories." One of the most useful tools for this necessary research is Rand McNally's *Campground & Trailer Park Directory*. It is readily available at sporting goods stores and outdoor equipment shops—even at many bookstores and newsstands. The National edition is a pretty thick book, but there are East and West regional editions that are smaller and less expensive. Your local library probably has a copy at the Reference Desk.

A campground directory such as the Rand McNally will give you a lot of information about most of the camps located in the area you want to visit; such information as the size of the campground, the types of campsites available, the type of bath and toilet facilities, sport and recreation activities that are available, and the costs. It generally will show whether reservations are necessary and where to write or telephone for more specific information.

If you're going on a longer camping trip (those that we call a "camp and go" vacation—when you camp at different places as you tour an area), then such a campground directory is a necessary part of your equipment.

SOME CAMPGROUNDS ARE RIGHT OUTSIDE THE BIG CITY.

CAMP TRAILER

STRAP COOLER   LANTERN

5. *WHAT EQUIPMENT DO YOU NEED?*

If you're going to a group camp or a special-interest camp, the kind of equipment you'll need will depend upon the camp itself —and they probably will tell you what to bring. The instructions I've seen from group camps not only tell you what you *must* bring, but also suggest other things that would be nice to have along to make your stay more enjoyable. There is also a basic list in the Appendix.

Family camping is a different matter. Here you're on your own, and if you fail to plan ahead, you may have problems in camp. Too much gear will weigh you down; you'll spend your time messing with a lot of stuff you don't need. But if you don't take enough, you may find that you can't do the things you have to do or want to do. So planning your equipment needs is important.

The kind of camping you're going to do and where you're going to do it will largely determine what equipment you need. My wife and I have camped with little more than a pup tent, two sleeping bags, and our cooking utensils. For several years, we and our kids used a big tent-trailer that allowed us to bring anything we wanted, including a lot of stuff we didn't need. And we once went out in a friend's motor home, complete with air conditioning, microwave oven, television, and shower—although that wasn't really camping.

Since there is such a wide range of possibilities and since you'll want to plan each trip separately, let's talk about what would be needed by the imaginary Smith family for a summer weekend camping trip to a nearby wooded lake shore. Then we'll suggest additions they might consider for longer trips, trips to different places, or at different times of the year.

29

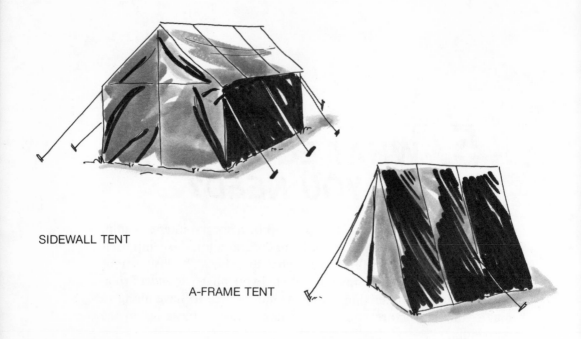

SIDEWALL TENT

A-FRAME TENT

For Shelter

The Smiths, of course, will have to have some kind of a shelter. Since they have two small children with them, they've chosen a 9′ × 12′ tent with vertical side walls. This is perhaps a bit larger than they really need, but it will give the children room to walk about inside—an important consideration if it rains. It also gives the parents stand-up room for dressing. And it's small enough to be erected comfortably by two people. The tent they chose has external aluminum support poles, which makes the inside area more usable since it isn't cluttered up with a center support pole.

There are, however, dozens of different styles, sizes, and qualities of tents on the market today. There are small pup tents—sort of portable A-frames—for one, two, or four people. There are side-wall tents that will sleep anywhere from four to eight. There are round tents, hexagonal tents, tents shaped like geodesic domes, tents with two rooms, tents with porches. Most tents today are made of very light material. They fold up into very small bundles and are easily packed and carried. Most smaller tents are free-standing; that is, they will stand upright without guy wires pegged into the ground around them. The support poles are lightweight metal and are easily erected. Some have double roofs—separate water-repellent rain flys permitting the roof of the tent itself to be made of a "breathable" material for better ventilation.

Since there are so many kinds of tents on the market, at widely varying prices, it's best to visit an outdoor equipment store and get acquainted with the possibilities. Or you could write to one of the companies listed in the Appendix and ask for a catalog. The Campmor and L.L. Bean catalogs have a wide range of equipment and will give you a pretty good idea of the range of prices.

However, spend some time deciding what tent to carry. Ask yourself the appropriate questions. How many people will use it? Will you have to spend time in it if it rains? Will you have to dress and undress in it? The answers to these questions will tell you how large a tent you need. But if there is a question in your mind, choose bigger. Nothing will put a damper on a camping trip quicker than having a tent that is too small for the people using it.

Tent-trailers have become increasingly popular. They are, as the name implies, tents on wheels—but some of them are pretty fancy. They range from very simple little "boxes" out of which unfolds a tent capable of sleeping two people, to very large trailers capable of sleeping six or eight people. Some have propane stoves, refrigerators, furnaces—even a kitchen sink. And recently they have included air conditioning. Tent-trailers are quite expensive, but they can be rented in most cities at a rather modest cost.

For long camping trips, where you intend to cover a considerable distance, a tent-trailer has a number of advantages. Setting up the camp takes only a few minutes, since everything is inside the trailer. When you're traveling, you can wait until later in the afternoon to make camp. And when it rains, the tent-trailer offers more space and the comfort of a cooking area inside, with a table for eating and table games. Breaking camp in the morning is quick and easy, letting you get on the road again quickly.

For most people, however, *real* camping means a tent. But choose your tent carefully. It may be wise for your first camping trip to rent a tent and some of the other equipment. In most areas, there are rental places that will rent you most of the basic "big price" equipment you will need. This could give you a chance to find out what kind of camping you like before you make the investment in your own equipment.

For Sleeping

The Smiths bought four sleeping bags designed to keep them comfortable even at about 32 °F. Since they bought good quality bags that will last a long time, they purchased full-size bags for the children. They also bought inflatable air mattresses for under the sleeping bags. They could have gotten foam pads, but the air mattresses when deflated are easier to pack. They also could have purchased small cots of aluminum and canvas, but they like the idea of sleeping on the ground.

As with tents, there are several different styles of sleeping bags, designed for a wide range of weather conditions. And the costs vary considerably, as you can imagine. If you're going to camp out in the open in cold weather, you'll need a bag designed to keep you warm at the lowest temperature to be expected. A down-filled bag to keep you warm well below zero can cost nearly $200. If you're going to camp only in summer and in a tent or a cabin, you can get by with a much less expensive bag. Think about the kinds of camping you intend to do before you get your bag, and then get one designed for your kind of camping. If you don't "sleep warm," you won't enjoy camping.

For Making Camp

The Smiths will need a certain amount of miscellaneous camp gear to make their camp. They'll need:

- *A supply of small rope or cord for hanging things—clothes to dry, food out of the reach of varmints, etc. (A supply of line is the handiest thing in camp.)*
- *Ax or hatchet for cutting wood*
- *Sharp sheath knife or folding hunting knife for all sorts of things*
- *Container for carrying and storing water*
- *Container for holding trash and garbage (Good campers dispose of all of their trash, leaving a clean campsite.)*
- *Camp lantern*
- *Good flashlight*
- *Matches in a waterproof box*
- *Insect repellent*
- *First-aid kit (More about this later.)*

Each camper should develop a personal list of this type of equipment, depending on the specific type of camping being planned.

For Cooking and Eating

The Smiths are camping at an established campsite that has a camping table with side benches and a stone fireplace as permanent fixtures. A supply of wood is available at the camp. Their necessary cooking and eating equipment, therefore, is pretty simple. They have to bring their cooking utensils, plates, silverware, and so on, but they don't have to worry about a stove or fuel. They will find it handy to have a dining fly—a sort of canopy over the camp table for shelter from rain and sun.

For their cooking utensils, they have purchased an aluminum camp set, such as those made by Mirro Corporation. These are available for from two to six people and contain a coffee pot, plates, cups, and two or three pails that double as cooking pots. The whole combination stores in the largest pot, and the lid doubles as a frying pan. The Smiths also need an ice chest and an insulated water container. An inexpensive set of stainless steel knives, forks, and spoons, a couple of knives for preparing food, and a long-handled fork for cooking complete the necessary equipment.

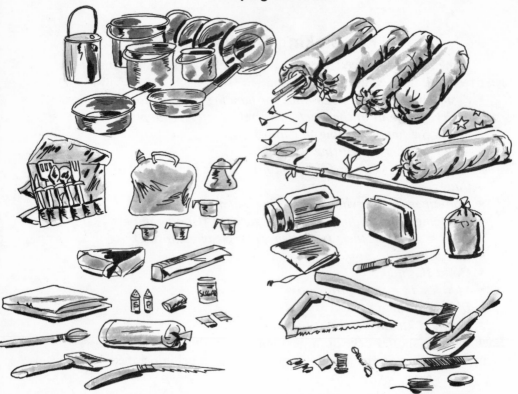

Actually, the cooking equipment in camp can range from the primitive to the elaborate—from a wooden spit for holding food over an open fire to a propane three-burner cooking stove with grill and oven. And the eating facilities can range from sitting on a log with a tin plate on your knees to the comfort of a folding aluminum camp table with a canopy. Since most established camping areas are equipped with tables and fireplaces, the equipment described for the Smith family is really all that is absolutely necessary. But you can get as elaborate as you want.

In addition to the essentials indicated for the Smith family, my family takes along a Coleman gas stove for cooking food when it's raining and the wood is wet. And for cooking over the open fire, we use a wire rack over the fireplace. On our longer trips, we also take a fireplace griddle because pancakes in the morning are delicious. We also like a cast-iron skillet better than the aluminum one that comes with the camp set.

We also take spatulas, tongs for fishing things out of the fire, food containers for holding food in the ice chest. And for salt and pepper and such, you can buy (or build) a camp "kitchen"—a box with a fold-down front and compartments inside for holding the things you need for cooking.

As you become a more experienced camper, you will learn just what additional equipment makes life in camp more comfortable and enjoyable, and will adjust the list accordingly. But the best advice is to start out light. When we first started camping, we carried enough equipment to support an army for a month. Gradually, as we learned that we really never used much of the stuff we carried, we tossed it out. Now our equipment list (and we do keep a check-off list so that we don't forget the things we really need) contains only the essentials. It's more fun that way—and we feel more like we're camping. After all, we want to get out into nature—not spend all our time caring for equipment we don't need.

For Recreation

In this category, we'll include all those things you do in camp other than eating and sleeping. Since we don't know what the Smiths' interests are, we don't know what recreational equipment they will want to take with them. Our imaginary family is on its own here. So are you. The equipment you'll need will depend on what you want to do.

Aside from the very large items—such as a canoe or a fishing boat—here are some suggestions of things we've taken with us from time to time and found enjoyable:

- *Books and magazines*
- *Musical instruments*
- *Camera*
- *Table games, such as cards, checkers, Scrabble, Trivial Pursuit, etc.*
- *Baseball bat, gloves, and ball*
- *Fishing equipment*
- *Binoculars*
- *Bird, wild flower, and tree guidebooks*
- *Radio or cassette player—but don't annoy other campers with it*
- *Canteen*
- *Small knapsack*

Here, again, every camper will have a personal list of things to bring. You'll make your own list as you learn what things are most fun in camp.

For Hygiene

Since the Smiths are camping in an established campsite, there is a bathhouse with toilets, running water, and showers. They will, however, have to bring some things with them:

- *Toothpaste and toothbrushes*
- *Combs and hairbrushes*
- *Soap and shampoo*
- *Towels and washcloths*
- *Shaving equipment*
- *Dishpan and dishtowels*

For a weekend, that's about all they'll need. Longer trips and trips to more primitive campsites present different problems of hygiene. On longer trips, laundering of clothing often is necessary. And while some established camping areas have laundry equipment, many do not. Of course, primitive areas have none. Since you don't want to burden yourself with too many changes of clothing, you may want to carry some laundry soap. You can wash out some clothes in the largest of the cooking pots. (Don't use detergent in lakes or streams; it's bad for the fish. Use soap; it's biodegradable.)

Trips to primitive area campsites can present different problems. For these trips, you should have a small garden trowel. Many primitive areas have only pit toilets, so it is wise to carry your own toilet paper. Very primitive areas may not even have pit toilets, and that's when you'll need the trowel. Experienced campers in very primitive areas choose a specific "toilet area" well away from the camp itself and use the "cat-hole" system, digging a small hole with the trowel and burying the human waste.

A Basic Camping List

You'll come up with your own list after you've camped a couple of times, but here's a basic list for the different kinds of camping. You can add your own special items to it.

For Group and Theme Camps
- Sleeping bag or blankets
- Extra clothing (depending on weather)
- Towel and washcloth, unless provided
- Toothbrush and toothpaste
- Comb, shampoo, and soap
- Emergency kit, including needle and thread, buttons, safety pins
- Flashlight
- Pocketknife
- Small soft backpack
- Mosquito repellent
- Hiking shoes or sneakers
- Raincoat
- Camera and film
- Special equipment the camp asks you to bring; i.e., swimsuit, sports equipment, etc.

Family Camping
- All of the preceding, plus:
- Tent
- Air or foam mattresses
- Dining fly
- Small rope supply
- Axe or hatchet
- Matches (waterproof box)
- Container for water
- Camp lantern
- Trash containers

- Dishpan, dishcloth, and towels
- Cooking utensils
  - Cooking pots
  - Skillet
  - Coffeepot
  - Cooking spoon
  - Cooking fork
  - Spatula
  - Large knife
- **Eating utensils**
  - Plates
  - Cups
  - Knives, forks, and spoons
- Camp stove
- Box for condiments
- Salt, pepper, sugar, etc.
- Ice chest
- Books
- Musical instrument(s)
- Table games (cards, etc.)
- Fishing gar
- Binoculars
- Bird books, etc.
- Canteen for hikes
- Radio
- Good hiking boots
- Laundry soap
- Small trowel
- Toilet paper
- First-aid kit
- Compass
- Map of the area
- Whistle

That's a basic list. Special trips—such as winter camping—will require other equipment, but this list will get you started. You can add to it from your own experience. Each list is different. But make a list and check it off before you go camping! It is very disappointing to get to camp and find you left some essential equipment at home.

6. WHAT ABOUT CLOTHING?

Since the Smiths are camping in the summer at a nearby lake, their clothing needs are rather simple. In addition to their ordinary clothing, they should take:

- *Swimsuits*
- *Sturdy walking shoes*
- *Light jacket*
- *Raincoat or poncho*
- *Extra socks*

For longer trips and for trips in colder weather or into the high mountains, different clothing demands will arise. On longer trips, it's harder to predict the weather. You'll want to be ready for whatever weather you're apt to encounter. For cold-weather camping or mountain camping where cold weather is always a possibility even in the middle of summer, you must be prepared. In addition to being sure that your sleeping bag and tent are suitable for the colder weather, you should have available:

- *Heavy jacket*
- *Warm gloves*
- *Warm cap that covers ears*
- *Face mask*
- *Thermal underwear*
- *Light sweater (You want to be able to "peel in layers" as the temperature rises.)*
- *More extra socks*

A PROPANE GAS STOVE IS A FAVORITE
OF CAMPERS FOR COOKING.

Cold-weather camping can be an exciting experience, but it also can be dangerous. Plan your trip with care. Don't try to take too many clothes, but take the right clothes.

For any camping other than the most casual, you will need good shoes or boots. If you're going to do any serious hiking, then invest in the best hiking boots you can afford. And break them in before you go. A pair of new boots can be very uncomfortable; you don't want blisters when you're camping.

For forest camping, take trousers of some hard-surface cloth such as whipcord or denim; it doesn't snag on underbrush. Also, take a hat for protection against both rain and sun. In woodsy areas, a narrow brim or a baseball cap is good; underbrush doesn't knock it off so easily. Wool shirts will keep you warm when they're wet. And take a very light nylon windbreaker—the kind you can wad up and stuff in your pocket. Again, make your own list, but make it to fit the camping you'll be doing.

7. WHAT ABOUT HEALTH AND PHYSICAL CONDITION?

Basic Requirements

People in reasonably good health should have no concern about camping. It need not be a strenuous activity, but it can be strenuous if you choose. That's one of the joys of camping. It *can* be just about anything you want it to be.

Most group camps and special-interest camps will require young people to have a physical exam before arriving at the camp. That is so the camp directors will be aware of any special needs of the campers and also avoid, if possible, the spreading of any communicable diseases.

For family camping, the rule should be that you don't go camping if you're not feeling well. Camping should be a fun experience; you'll not have fun if you're sick. Also, it would be more difficult to get proper medical attention if you're in a campsite far from a telephone and adequate medical facilities.

On the other hand, some types of camping definitely require special physical conditioning. If your camping trip is to include mountain climbing or long hikes or serious canoeing, for example, you'll want to work yourself into the proper physical condition for the activity. Don't try it cold turkey; you're apt to wind up with some very sore muscles and spoil the rest of your trip. As with any sport or any physical demand you place on your body, get in condition before you try it. You'll have more fun.

Camping for the Handicapped

Camping is fun for the handicapped, too. Many people with physical handicaps camp regularly and enjoy it perhaps more than those for whom a wider range of day-to-day physical activity is possible. Maybe the biggest handicap for those physically less able is the belief that they *can't* do something. But I've seen people enjoying camp in a wheelchair. And I've gone hiking with someone who uses a cane and has to be helped occasionally over difficult places.

Camping is for anyone who loves the out-of-doors, who enjoys natures and wants to learn more about it, who wants to become more self-reliant. A physical handicap is no bar to any of those things. And going camping with someone handicapped can be especially rewarding if you can help another person enjoy an experience otherwise not possible.

Safety

Safety should be one of the first things anyone learns about camping and one of the skills that is practiced always. Camping can be dangerous if you're not careful. You can fall and turn an ankle. You can cut yourself with an ax while chopping wood. You can encounter poison ivy. You can capsize your canoe. You can burn yourself while cooking over a campfire. You can get a sunburn or a frostbite. You could even start a forest fire!

A good first-aid kit is an absolute necessity in camp. It doesn't have to be fancy or even very expensive, but it should have at least these essential items:

- Bandages
- Band-Aids
- Gauze compresses
- Cotton swabs
- Adhesive tape
- Scissors
- Sterile pads
- Antiseptic

If you have no knowledge of first aid, then a good preparation for serious camping, particularly if you plan to go into wilderness, would be to see if you can take a short first-aid course. Some Red Cross chapters offer such courses, as do many local fire departments, police departments, and municipal recreation departments.

Think safety! Know your limitations. Know how to use the equipment you take with you, use it wisely, and keep it in good condition. When hiking in unfamiliar territory, have a compass with you and know how to use it. Insist that those with you follow safe practices. If you use a boat or canoe, for instance, be sure there are life jackets and that everyone uses them. Be careful. An accident in a remote camp can be far more serious than the same occurrence at home. You'll be in strange surroundngs and possibly far from adequate medical insurance.

Here are some safety suggestions:

- *Never camp alone without leaving a "flight plan" with someone, indicating just where you're going and when you will return.*
- *Be careful with campfires. Keep a container of water near your campfire.*
- *When you hike, carry a compass, a map, and a whistle. If lost, you can use the map and compass. If injured, use the whistle to call for help.*
- *Learn to use the map and compass, and never hike unfamiliar territory before first studying the terrain and noting prominent geographic features that will help you orient yourself. Note which direction the streams run.*
- *If you're hiking in primitive areas, learn to recognize the edible plants and berries of the area for emergencies.*
- *Follow the old Boy Scout rule: Be prepared! Plan ahead! Think safety!*

8. WHERE TO GET MORE INFORMATION

Now that you've had a brief introduction to some of the basics of camping, you may want to learn more about the possibilities.

Through the earlier parts of this book, I've suggested places for you to get more information about specific areas of the subject of camping. You'll find the addresses of a number of such places in the Appendix that follows. But you'll have to ask the questions. You'll find, however, that camping people are friendly people, and they like to get others into the camping habit, too. They'll not only answer your questions, they'll help you in areas you haven't yet thought to ask about.

Your local outdoor equipment store is a good place to start. After all, they make their living selling the things you need to go camping. You're a potential customer. But don't overlook the state and federal government agencies. Your parents' taxes support those agencies; use their services.

Every state has a department that deals with outdoor recreation, including camping. The department may be called the Department of Conservation or Recreation or Tourism; one state calls it the Department of Highways. All states have such a department. Find out what it is and write to ask for information about the camping facilities in state parks, state forests, and other state-supervised areas. You'll find that there are more such places in your state than you dreamed of.

The Department of the Interior in Washington, D.C., controls the National Park Service; the Department of Agriculture runs the U.S. Forest Service; both operate campgrounds. You can write to them for information about campgrounds they operate, or you can write to the Superintendent of Documents in Washington, D.C., for a catalog of the available camping area documents. See the Appendix for addresses of these agencies.

You can write directly to any of the companies that market camping equipment. Most have a public relations department that will send you catalogs and descriptions of their products. They like to do that, since they make their money selling such equipment, and you're a potential customer.

As suggested earlier, your local library is a good place to get more information. They will have books on specific types of camping listed in the card catalog. The Reference Desk will have a number of reference works that can help you. For example, there is an *Index of Organizations* that will give you the addresses and a description of the activities and publications of organizations interested in camping activities. The Reference Librarian can show you how to use it.

Why not start now? Find out what you can about the particular kind of camping you want to do. Then, *go camping!*

APPENDIX

Listed below are a few publications and organizations that can give you more information about camping and camps. There are many other publications, books, and organizations that you can find out about from your local library, but this list will get you started.

Directories

Campground & Trailer Park Directory
Rand McNally & Company
Campground Publications
PO Box 728
Skokie, IL 60076
(a very comprehensive directory; widely available; has national and regional editions.)

Peterson's *Summer Opportunities for Kids and Teenagers*
Peterson's Guides, Inc.
Princeton, NJ 08540
(lists camps, programs, activities, costs, etc.)

Woodall's *National Campground Directory*
Simon & Schuster
1230 Ave. of the Americas
New York, NY 10020
(also publishes regional editions.)

Organizations

American Camping Association
Bradford Woods
Martinsville, IN 46151
(publishes "Camping" and "Parents' Guide to Accredited Camps")

National Campers and Hikers Association
7172 Transit Rd.
Buffalo, NY 14221
(has regional information centers; publishes "Tent and Trail")

YWCA
135 W. 50th St.
New York, NY 10020

YMCA
101 N. Wacker Dr.
Chicago, IL 60606

Camp Fire, Inc.
4601 Madison Ave.
Kansas City, MO 64112
(formerly called Camp Fire Girls, it's now for boys, too)

YM-YWHA
1395 Lexington Ave.
New York, NY 10028

Girl Scouts of the USA
830 Third Ave.
New York, NY 10022

Boy Scouts of America
1325 Walnut Hill Ln.
Irving, TX 75062

Sierra Club
PO Box 7959
San Francisco, CA 94120

Appalachian Mountain Club
5 Joy St.
Boston, MA 02108

National Parks and Forests

Office of Public Affairs
National Park Service   Room 3043
Department of the Interior
Washington, D.C. 20240

Recreation Department
U.S. Forest Service
Department of Agriculture
Washington, D.C. 20013

Superintendent of Documents
Government Printing Office
North Capital & H Streets, N.W.
Washington, D.C. 20402

Equipment Manufacturers

Campmor
810 Route 17 North
PO Box 999
Paramus, NJ 07653
(all kinds of camping equipment—will send large catalog)

Mirro Corporation
PO Box 409
Manitowoc, WI 54220
(good camp cooking equipment)

Eureka Company
PO Box 966
Binghamton, NY 1390
(my favorite tents—all sizes)

King Seeley Thermos Co.
Thermos Division
Norwich, CN 06360
(variety of camp equipment)

Nalge Company
Special Products Dept.
PO Box 365
Rochester, NY 14602
(good camp containers for food and liquid)

The Coleman Company, Inc.
445 North Minnesota
Wichita, KA 67214
(a wide variety of good camping equipment)

AlpineAire Products
PO Box 926
Nevada City, CA 95959
(good freeze-dried foods for hiking and camping)

There are many other companies manufacturing camping equipment and supplies, and new companies join the market al the time. Also, new technology is being applied to camping equipment, as to everything else, and new and sometimes better items are introduced all the time. The best way to keep up with what is available is to visit an outdoor equipment store from time to time.

Books

There are a great many other books on camping. You can find them listed in your local library. But the best how-to-do-it manual I know of is the *Official Boy Scout Handbook*. (The Girl Scouts have a similar handbook, but the Boy Scout book is the one I'm familiar with.) This book, now in its ninth edition, has sold over 31,000,000 copies since it was first printed in 1910—which makes it a real best seller. It covers all aspects of camping and many other subjects as well—safety, hygiene, first aid, plant and animal recognition, compass and map reading, and so on. It can be purchased from any Scout council headquarters (which you'll find listed in the telephone directory under Boy Scouts of America) for about $5.00, and I'd recommend it for any person about to go camping for the first time.

Index